The Allan Wells Book of Sprinting

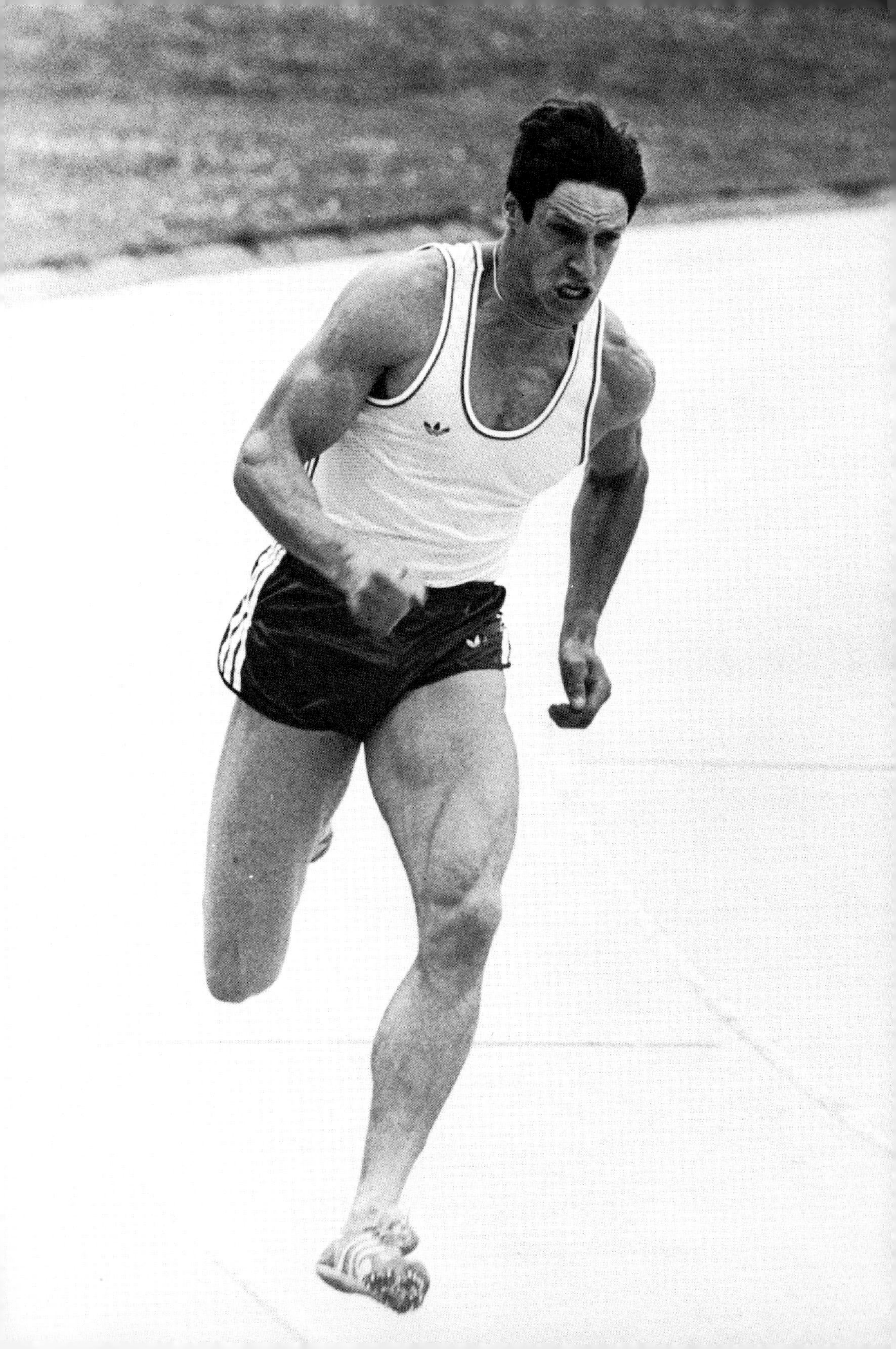

The Allan Wells Book of Sprinting

Margot Wells

EP Publishing Limited

Copyright © Margot Wells 1983

ISBN 0 7158 0842 7 (casebound)
      0 7158 0843 5 (paperback)

British Cataloguing in Publication Data
Wells, Margot
    Allan Wells book of sprinting.
    1. Sprinting
    I. Title
    796.4'26   GV1069
      ISBN 0–7158–0842–7
      ISBN 0–7158–0843–5 Pbk

First edition 1983

Published by EP Publishing Limited, Bradford Road, East Ardsley, Wakefield, West Yorkshire, WF3 2JN, England

Text set in 11/13pt Times New Roman by The Word Factory, Rossendale

Printed and bound in Italy by Legatoria Editoriale Giovanni Olivotto, Vicenza

Design: Giolitto, Wrigley & Couch Design Partnership

Photographs
Allsport/Tony Duffy, pages 44, 88
Werner Schulze, page 7
All other photographs by Chris Smith

This book is copyright under the Berne Convention. All rights are reserved. Apart from any fair dealing for the purposes of private study, research, criticism or review, as permitted under the Copyright Act, 1956, no part of this publication may be reproduced, stored in a retrieval system, or transmitted in any form or by any means, electronic, electrical, chemical, mechanical, optical, photocopying, recording or otherwise, without the prior written permission of the copyright owner. Enquiries should be addressed to the publishers.

Contents

	Profile of Allan Wells	6
1	An athletic biography	9
2	The basics of sprinting	15
3	Preparation and warm-up	18
	Food	18
	Clothing	19
	Warm-up	21
4	Technique	43
	Arm and leg action	43
	Bend running	55
	The start and the finish	55
5	Training	65
	General training methods	65
	Sprint training for women	85
6	The mental approach	89
	An interview with Allan Wells	93

Profile of Allan Wells

Name:	Allan W. Wells
Date of birth:	3 May, 1952
Birthplace:	Edinburgh
Height:	6ft 0in (1.83m)
Weight:	176lb (80kg)
Schools:	Fernieside Primary and Liberton High School
Club:	Edinburgh Southern Harriers
Married:	Yes — wife's name is Margot
Pets:	Persian cat: 'Gabi'
Car:	Sunbeam Lotus
Favourite food:	Steak and Baked Alaska
Favourite country:	Germany
Hobbies:	Do-it-yourself; model making; fast cars
Likes:	Running fast; good food; warm weather
Dislikes:	Competing on cold, wet days; bad timekeeping

Allan after his moment of triumph in Moscow

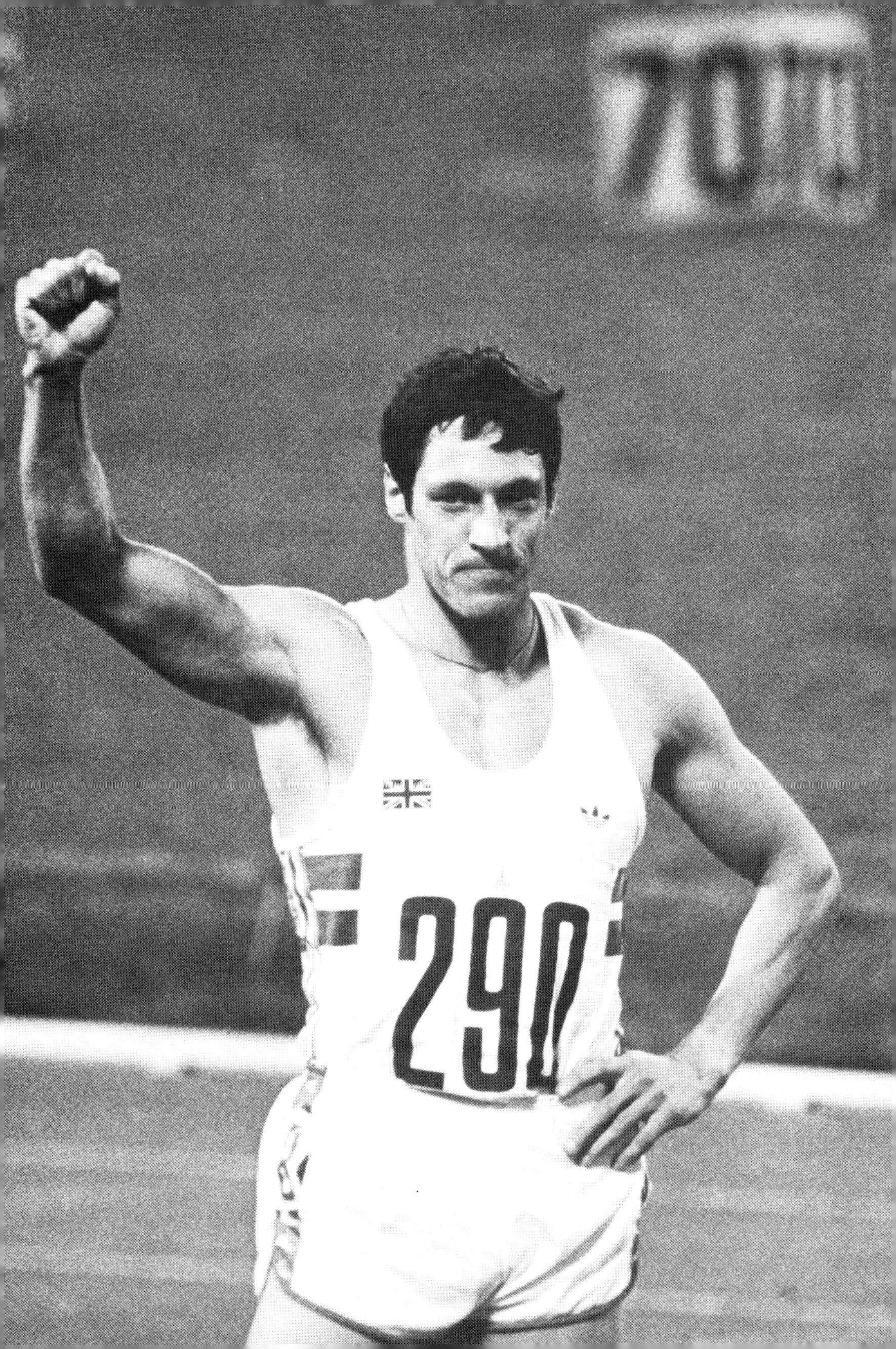
290

CHAPTER ONE

An athletic biography

Fernieside Crescent in Edinburgh must be one of the few streets in the world that can boast of having produced *two* Olympic athletes: both Chris Black and Allan Wells were brought up within fifty yards of each other, overlooking Edinburgh Southern Harriers track. As a child Allan often used to watch the club train at the local track and, on more than one occasion, became the object of their races through shouting comments at the athletes!

Allan entered his first race at the tender age of six, while he was at Fernieside Primary School. He came second in the 60 yards at the Edinburgh Scholastics Competition at Meadowbank — not the new Meadowbank but the original stadium which stood on the same site. However, it was at Liberton High School that Allan became really interested in sport. He enjoyed football, basketball, badminton and cross-country running, as well as track and field; and although he was not particularly interested in academic work he had a leaning towards practical work and technical subjects which is still reflected in his interests today. Allan's major victory while at school was winning the Scottish Under-15 Long-Jump title, although he also competed in the sprints, long jump, triple jump and cross-country.

At this time Allan was also a member of the 9th Edinburgh Boys' Brigade Company and he enjoyed the sporting aspects of this movement. He represented the Brigade in athletics, cross-country, football, badminton and gymnastics. His greatest success was in the cross-country when he won the Scottish Brigade Championships.

Allan decided to concentrate wholly on athletics at the age of 17. Being a bit of a loner, he enjoyed the pressures of an individual sport rather than team games where he had to rely on other people as well as himself. This decision, made at a relatively young age, showed how

AN ATHLETIC BIOGRAPHY

much he enjoyed taking pressure, and this is a major factor in his world-class performances today.

He started his career as a triple- and long-jumper, and progressed slowly through the ranks until a foot injury, which required an operation on his toe, temporarily halted his progress. Not one to lie down to this, he was soon training again with one leg in plaster! He required two new plasters — one he fell on and cracked, and another went mouldy with sweat — before the plaster was able to be removed for good. It took a lot of hard work and courage to come back as the leg and foot were left very weak and a one-hundred-metre jog was a major effort.

Allan's first major success in triple jumping came when he won the Scottish Junior Triple-Jump title. His progress was not spectacular; in fact he does not appear in the Scottish ranking list until 1971.

Event	*Year*	*Personal best*	*Age*
Triple jump	1970	12.95 metres	18
Long jump	1970	6.65 metres	18

It is worth noting that David Jenkins led the junior rank in the 100-metres and 200-metres with times of 10.6 and 21.1 s. Allan Wells did not rank in the first sixteen!

Event	*Year*	*Personal best*	*Age*
100-metres	1971	11.1 seconds	19
Long jump	1971	6.73 metres	19

(Comment: Allan Wells has real ability and promises much for the future!)

Triple jump	1971	13.27 metres	19

The above performances took place while Allan was still a junior.

In 1972 at the Bells Indoor Sports Centre in Perth Allan won the 50-metres in 6.2 s, the 300-metres in 37.1 s and the long jump. His performances proved that he had sprinting qualities in need of harnessing and pointing in the right direction.

Event	Year	Personal best	Age
100-metres	1972	10.9 seconds	20
200-metres	1972	22.1 seconds	20
400-metres	1972	49.2 seconds	20
Long jump	1972	7.32 metres	20

This was to be Allan's best year in athletics until 1976.

Event	Year	Personal best	Age
Long jump	1973	7.30 metres	21
Long jump	1974	7.20 metres	22
Long jump	1975	7.15 metres	23
400-metres	1975	49.7 seconds	23

Although Allan gained several Scottish International vests in the long jump, his 1972 jump of 7.32 m was to be his life-time best. While long jump was his main event, he also dabbled in the sprints for his club but, as the lists show, he could not manage any faster than 10.9 s for the 100-metres — and even that was wind-assisted! However, he did show some of his hidden talent while running the first leg of the 4 × 100-metres relay; he was rarely overtaken during these runs, which were against some formidable opposition.

In February 1976 Allan decided to concentrate on sprinting. He had seen friends improve dramatically after changing their training programme to a more disciplined style involving the use of the speedball, and felt that this method of training would suit him. He therefore settled down to train as a sprinter convinced he could become, at worst, a Great-Britain internationalist.

He started the season with a 10.9-second run on a cinder track into the wind — a personal best at the time — and produced a season's and life-time's best of 10.55 s in the 100-metres at Crystal Palace with a following wind of 0.5, thus running the best legal time in Britain that year. His best in the 200-metres was 21.42 (21.2 hand timing) at Meadowbank, but he did manage to gain a Great Britain International vest in the 4 × 100-metres against Canada.

In 1977, although not improving on his 10.55, he had some very fast runs into the wind — e.g. 10.7 s with a minus 4.3 wind at Meadow-

AN ATHLETIC BIOGRAPHY

bank. He also had two windy 10.4-second runs at Meadowbank. His improvement in the 200-metres was much more significant with two legal 20.9-second runs and a 21.6 s into a minus 4.2 wind.

In 1978 he broke slightly from his hitherto strict routine, and added some of his own ideas on training; this paid off handsomely in the Commonwealth Games in Edmonton. He started the season late owing to a problem with shin soreness, and then all his early runs were into the wind and so little notice was taken of them. He ran 10.4 s into a minus 1.7 wind at Birmingham and 10.50 s (a legal personal best) into a minus 2.2 wind in Athens. However, it was on 9 July at Gateshead that Britain realised they had a potential world-class sprinter. Allan Wells ran against Don Quarrie, James Sandford and James Gilkes and achieved 10.29 s with a following wind of 0.5 to equal the 20-year-old British record of Peter Radford — and he did it putting his hands in the air five metres from the line.

The following week at Meadowbank he finally obliterated the earlier record from the books with a time of 10.15 s (with a plus wind of 1.3). He also showed considerable improvement in the 200-metres before leaving for the Commonwealth Games, with a run of 20.70 s into a 4.1 wind; this indicated that the British 200-metres record of 20.66 s was also under threat. At the Games Allan produced his best running to finish second in the 100-metres in a windy 10.07 s and to win the 200-metres in an equally windy 20.12 s (he did beat the British record in the second round, easing up). This was really his first break into world-class sprinting, but he did not have the experience to cope with the European Championships which came only four weeks later, where he could finish only a very tired sixth.

With no big Games in 1979 Allan progressed steadily through the season with a 10.27 s into a minus 0.7 wind in Bremen and a 10.19 s with plus 1.3 wind at the Europa Cup Final in Turin. He was third in this race, mainly due to slipping at the start, and was beaten by Mennea and Worinin. In the 200-metres at Bremen he ran a new British record of 20.56 s while suffering from a virus infection and then in the Europa Cup Final went on to run a 20.29 s with a wind of 2.2, just over the legal limit, to beat Pietro Mennea and become the first European for six years to beat the Italian — and in Italy! The 1979 season climaxed with Allan finishing second to James Sandford in the Golden Sprint in Zurich. Allan's combined time of 10.22 + 20.42

12

AN ATHLETIC BIOGRAPHY

(equalling 30.64 s) gave him second place overall. His 20.42 s was a new British record and was run into a minus 1.9 wind.

The Olympic Games were overshadowed by withdrawals, allegations and politics but in no way did this detract from Allan's performance at the Games. Allan had very few races before the Games; his best times were a 10.05 and a 20.05 s on a very cold windy day at Meadowbank. Then in Moscow, owing to some peculiar seeding, he had to run a new British record of 10.11 s in the second round. The final was a hard-fought affair with Allan getting the decision in 10.25 s into a wind of minus 1.1. The 200-metres was a test of endurance; having just run four rounds of the 100-metres, he then had to start all over again and run four rounds of the 200-metres. This took its toll both physically and mentally and although he ran a new British record of 20.21 s it was only good enough for the silver medal. On returning from the Games, Allan spent a tiring week in Europe, but he still managed to beat all those who had not participated in the Olympic Games and who were still fresh and full of running.

His finest year to date must be 1981. After an indifferent start to the season he produced scintillating form, running a 10.17 s into a minus 0.9 wind to win the 100-metres in the Europa Cup Final. Owing to a bad lane draw, he finished second in the 200-metres in 20.35 s with a plus 0.3 wind. Then, on a cold, wet and windy evening in Berlin, Allan showed the world he was not a spent force by returning 10.15 s (wind plus 2.3) and 20.15 s (wind plus 2.5) to gain an aggregate of 30.30 s and win the Golden Sprint title — and with it the title of 'the fastest man in the world'.

Between this event and the World Cup Allan picked up a stomach bug but still managed to win the 100-metres in 10.20 s. In the 200-metres, realising that he had lost first place, he cantered home, just making sure of second place.

On page 14 is a table of his best results to date. Even now, at the age of thirty, he believes there are still faster times to come.

AN ATHLETIC BIOGRAPHY

Event	Match	Place	Time	Wind (m/s)	Place	Age
100-metres	Invitation	Gateshead	10.29	+0.5	1st	26
100-metres	British Championships	Meadowbank	10.15	+1.3	1st	26
100-metres	Commonwealth Games	Edmonton	10.07	+7.5	2nd	26
200-metres	Commonwealth Games	Edmonton	20.12	+4.3	1st	26
100-metres	Europa Cup Final	Turin	10.19	+1.3	3rd	27
200-metres	Europa Cup Final	Turin	20.29	+2.2	1st	27
{100-metres 200-metres}	Golden Sprint	Zurich	10.22+ 20.42	−0.1 −1.9	2nd	27
100-metres	Olympic Games	Moscow	10.25	−1.1	1st	28
200-metres	Olympic Games	Moscow	20.21	nil	2nd	28
100-metres	Europa Cup Final	Zagreb	10.17	−0.9	1st	29
200-metres	Europa Cup Final	Zagreb	20.35	+0.3	2nd	29
{100-metres 200-metres}	Golden Sprint	Berlin	10.15+ 20.15	+2.3 +2.5	1st	29
100-metres	World Cup	Rome	10.20	?	1st	29
200-metres	World Cup	Rome	20.53	?	2nd	29
100-metres	Commonwealth Games	Brisbane	10.02	+5.9	1st	30
200-metres	Commonwealth Games	Brisbane	20.43	+0.4	1st eq.	30

CHAPTER TWO

The basics of sprinting

If we look back on the careers of our top jumpers, throwers and distance runners we will probably find that they were nearly all failed sprinters. In other words they all had speed, which is an essential ingredient in all athletic performances, be it putting the shot or outkicking the field in the 1,500-metres. The amount of speed the athlete has dictates which event he or she will eventually specialise in. So why does everyone want to be a sprinter?

Sprinting has a charisma about it which is in some way mystical — no tactics, just sheer blinding speed. If we think back to our schooldays, the winner of the 100-metres was always looked upon as someone special, whereas the poor winner of the shot putt was always scorned for being the 'fattie'. No matter the quality of the performance of the athletes — the sprinter always came out tops. It is because of the charisma of the event that it is heralded as one of the blue-riband events in track and field today.

Many people believe that sprinters are born and not made; a statement we have heard many times over and one which, to a certain extent, has some truth. Natural ability plays a part in a sprinter's career, but it is rarely the record breakers at fifteen and sixteen who go on to become the world-class athletes of the future. It is the ones who were fifth and sixth on the list who emerge on top. Why? There is no secret formula for success. Athletes at the top have the same basic equipment as other people — namely, one head, two legs, two arms and a body. The magic ingredient — if there is one — is hard work. There are no short cuts, no magic wands. To me the unbeatable combination is a mixture of natural ability, a lot of hard work and the correct training techniques.

We will look at technique later on in the book, but first let us

THE BASICS OF SPRINTING

consider speed and discover what it is, how it is achieved and how you improve it. The dictionary definition of speed is given as 'ratio of distance covered to time taken by a moving body'. In other words, speed is all about covering a certain distance in as little time as possible. So now that we know what we have to do, how do we do it? The answer to that would appear to be fairly simple, in that all you have to do is to move your arms and legs as fast as you can in a straight line. By this means you would achieve your natural speed; but the last and most important factor, and what this book is really all about, is how to improve on what you have.

There are two ways in which to improve speed when sprinting:
(a) cadence rate (i.e. leg speed)
(b) stride length

In other words what a sprinter is trying to do is to move his arms and legs as fast as possible whilst at the same time taking as long a stride (and therefore fewer for the same distance) as he can.

Let us look at leg speed first, as this is the harder area to improve upon. There are lots of speed drills to improve cadence rate, and any sort of exercise which involves moving the arms and legs at maximum speed will help in achieving this. Note that the arms must be helped as well as the legs, otherwise what will happen is that your legs will be able to keep going at speed but your arms will tire and will not keep pace. The end result will be that your legs will slow down. The arms can dictate to the legs both the speed they move at and the direction they move in. Try it for yourself. Try and move your arms slowly and your legs fast, and then try and move your arms from side to side and keep your legs going in a straight line at speed — very nearly impossible.

The speedball, which I mentioned briefly in the introduction, is another aid to assisting cadence. The body has to be prepared in order to move at high speed; to do this, fast messages must first be sent along nerve pathways instructing the muscle to contract fully and frequently. Training in this is one of the uses of the speedball. The body moves at a far greater speed than it ever needs to during a race; and, therefore, it finds it easier to cope with the pace of a race. This tends also to reduce the injury risk, as the muscles will already have contracted at a far greater speed beforehand. (Speedball is discussed in greater detail in Chapter 5.)

THE BASICS OF SPRINTING

To improve the length of stride is in a way a far easier task. Again it can be split into two: (a) power (b) mobility.

(a) Power — This will be dealt with more fully in Chapter 5. If we can look at it in terms of a simple equation, its importance will become obvious. If one has 0.4kW of power to push 80kg of weight along a track and someone else has 0.8kW of power to push the same 80kg, the second person will push it twice as fast. Simple, but the difficulty is that a sprinter needs fast muscle power as opposed to slow, heavy power. Therefore one has to be very careful about the way one goes about becoming more powerful.

(b) Mobility — Again this will be dealt with in greater detail later. If your muscles are tight you will not be able to stretch out your legs, and the injury risk is increased by your being unable to relax and stride out.

At all times great care must be taken to minimise any injury risk; there is no point in being strong and fast but being unable to compete due to lack of stretching or insufficient care taken during training.

CHAPTER THREE

Preparation and warm-up

The preparation for a sprint race does not start the night before, but on the first day of training; and a lot depends on the life-style the athlete leads thereafter. There is a saying 'you cannot burn a candle at both ends' — well, an athlete cannot afford to burn a candle at all! Sleep is probably one of the most important factors governing an athlete's performance. If you go to bed late after a hard day's work and training, not only does your work suffer the next day, but your training suffers too as you are both mentally and physically tired. The problems do not stop there. Training goes on because it has to, and therefore there is an ongoing downhill situation with the body's resources being constantly drained. The amount of sleep you need varies from individual to individual, and each athlete will know how much he or she needs to be able to cope with living and training.

Food

Food is another important factor. The usual requirement is plenty of the right kind. The food balance is crucial because if too much of the wrong kind of food is eaten then the wrong kind of weight is gained (i.e. fat rather than muscle), upsetting the strength/weight ratio. Similarly, if not enough is eaten then weight and power are lost. So the right amount of food is essential to be able to train and build muscles which, in turn, will help you to run faster. It is natural to gain weight when training, as muscle develops, but do not go berserk — remember it gets a bit hard going propelling 100kg (224lb) along a 100-metre straight!

So what is the right kind of food? A cooked or good breakfast is essential, especially if you train twice a day. Fruit juice, cereal, eggs,

PREPARATION AND WARM-UP

toast and honey — or any combination of these — should suffice. Lunch should be a cooked meal if possible but, even if this is not practicable, the food should be substantial and not just a pie and a pint at the local. Another cooked meal after training, to replace lost calories, should round off one's eating for the day. Meals should be balanced, using meat, fish, chicken, potatoes, fresh fruit and vegetables, bread and cheese. Meals should be varied and appetising. Added vitamins have always been controversial, but by taking them at least you know you have covered all possibilities and will not lack anything. Other dietary ingredients which should not be neglected are electrolyte replenishment (e.g. salt) and minerals essential to the body's metabolism.

When to eat is almost as important as what to eat. It is as impossible to run on a full stomach as on an empty stomach. If you have nothing in your stomach then your body has nothing with which to replace used energy. It is up to the individual to work out for himself the ideal time to eat before a race, but the normal time it takes for a full meal to be digested is around three to four hours.

Clothing

Once the inside of the body has been taken care of, then we must take a look at the outside. An athlete's kit is as important in training as it is in competition. Training kit must always be fresh and clean — not only will it make the athlete feel better, but training companions will appreciate the gesture! One must wear enough clothes to be warm but not so many that free movement is hindered. Remember, it is easier to take items of clothing off if one is too warm than it is to add clothing if one is not warm enough. The basic essentials are a tracksuit or loose-fitting trousers and jumper, with waterproof covering if possible — even an old mackintosh is better than nothing.

If you can only afford to buy certain items then the first priority is your footwear. You can wear any kind of clothing to train in, but you must have the correct footwear, otherwise you will cause injuries to your feet which can stop you competing. Training shoes should be firm and fairly solid with good supporting areas within the shoe. Ideally two pairs of spikes should be purchased — one pair for competition and one pair for training. The competition spikes should

PREPARATION AND WARM-UP

An example of good footwear

Right: *Spikes worn by Allan in major competitions*

feel special and light when put on, compared with the training spikes which should be comfortable, supportive and fairly long-lasting. The same goes for running kit: if you have a special vest and shorts (maybe in your club colours) try not to wear them for training. This all adds to your well-being before a race. You feel different and look good. Although it will not necessarily turn you into a world-class sprinter, if you feel clean, healthy and a bit special, it certainly will help. When Allan won the Golden Sprints in 1981 it was a very cold, wet evening, but because he had three complete changes of clothing with him he always lined up wearing dry, warm clothes. This plays a large part in the feeling of well-being, especially if one's opponents are wearing wet clothes and shoes!

Warm-up

Once the athlete has prepared himself to run, what can he do to make himself ready immediately prior to a race? The warm-up is probably more important than the race itself because if the warm-up is not performed properly then the athlete cannot do himself justice when the race begins.

PREPARATION AND WARM-UP

pages 25, 26, 27
Allan never jogs during a warm-up! That may seem strange as 90 per cent of athletes jog two or three laps during a warm-up. So if not, why not? We feel that by doing strides, starting off slowly and gradually increasing in speed, he can still concentrate on his running technique by the same means as he would while sprinting, whereas if he jogged he would be unable to run in the same way. After striding, a lot of stretching and mobility work should then take place to prepare the body for the task ahead. The purpose of stretching is to take the muscles through a greater range than they have to achieve during a race; in this way the muscles are not being asked to do anything they have not done before. Stretching is also important because as the muscles become stronger they become tighter, and this tightness would restrict the length of stride if a strict mobility programme were not adhered to.

The general rule for stretching is to start at the top and work your way down:

pages 28, 29
1. Rolling the head — Rotate the head, passing through as large a circumference as possible in both directions.

page 30
2. Arm rotation — Keeping the arm straight and close to the ears, rotate the arm in both directions.

pages 31, 32
3. Hip circles — Using only the pelvic area, circle the hips in both directions, again passing through as large a circumference as possible. This exercise can be extended by circling the upper body as well and then extended further by using the arms as well so that the whole body moves in a circle.

pages 33, 34
4. Side bends — Keeping the legs straight and the body in alignment, slide the hand down the leg as far as possible. Repeat on the other side.

page 35
5. Calf stretches — Leaning against a wall, walk the feet out until it is difficult to keep the heels flat on the ground, and then alternately lift and lower the heels.

6. Lunges —

pages 36, 37
(a) With both feet facing forward, place one leg in front of the other, wide apart, and try to force the thigh of the back leg onto the ground while keeping the trunk upright. The front knee should be over the front foot, which should have the heel on the ground. Again this exercise should be done equally to both sides, each leg in turn in front of the other.

PREPARATION AND WARM-UP

    (b) The same exercise as (a) but with the back foot on its side, giving a completely different type of stretch. *pages 38, 39*

7. Hamstring stretches —
    (a) Lying on your back with both hands supporting the hips off the ground, alternately stretch out each leg with the other one in a relaxed position. *page 40*
    (b) Lying on your back, grasp one leg behind the knee with both hands and pull the knee into the chest. Slowly straighten the leg and then pull the toes downwards thus creating a good stretch up the back of the leg. Relax the leg afterwards by allowing the lower leg to flop. *page 41*

8. Hip circles — Bend the leg and draw it across the body, then, keeping the leg bent, open it up, before straightening and returning to the opposite leg, which remains straight throughout. This should look like a type of breast-stroke leg kick with one leg. *page 42*

These are only a few of the hundreds of exercises available, and everyone has their own favourites. The most important factor to remember is never to jerk stretching movements. The sequence of stretching is:

stretch – hold – relax – stretch – hold – relax.

The important areas to stretch as far as sprinters are concerned are (a) hips (b) abductors (c) hamstrings (d) shoulders. (a) and (b) are important because these are the restricting muscles in terms of stride length, (c) because these are sprinters' 'achilles heels' and seem to cause most problems, and (d) if the shoulders are tight then they limit the amount of drive from the arms.

This whole programme should take approximately thirty minutes and should then be followed by more strides, still in training shoes. The spikes should then be put on just before starting to do the practice starts. It is important that the spikes are not put on until this moment, nor should any articles of clothing be removed except in extremely hot conditions. Only too often do we see juniors warming up in spikes, wearing only a tee-shirt and shorts! The aim of a warm-up is to prepare the body, both physically and mentally, for the task ahead; this means not only raising the body temperature but warming up the muscles inside as well. It is no good warming up and then stripping off ten minutes before a race begins, as the body will soon cool down and become stiff even before you start.

PREPARATION AND WARM-UP

The entire warming-up procedure should take approximately forty to fifty minutes and this should immediately precede the start of the race. Sometimes, however, a race meeting will be running behind schedule, and it is therefore important continually to check the times of the races beforehand and to adjust your warm-up time accordingly. In major Games such as the Olympics, European, Commonwealth etc. the athletes must report in some cases as much as forty minutes before the start of the race, so that too has to be taken into consideration. The warm-up timing should be well-rehearsed beforehand; it is just as important not to warm up too early as it is not to be rushed.

On completion of the race the athlete must put on his track gear and remove his spikes immediately; failure to do so could result in a chill, stiffness or, even worse, an injury. Avoid the temptation to discuss the race with anyone before putting on warm clothing and doing a warm-down.

A warm-down is not quite so important to a sprinter as it is to a middle/long-distance runner, but even so it has a place in the finishing off of a race. Again, while most athletes jog, we go back to striding, but this time we decrease the speed of each stride as opposed to increasing it. It is important to return the pulse rate and body temperature to normal in order to prevent stiffness and a build-up of impurities in the muscles.

Above and following two pages:
Even during the warm-up Allan concentrates fully on technique

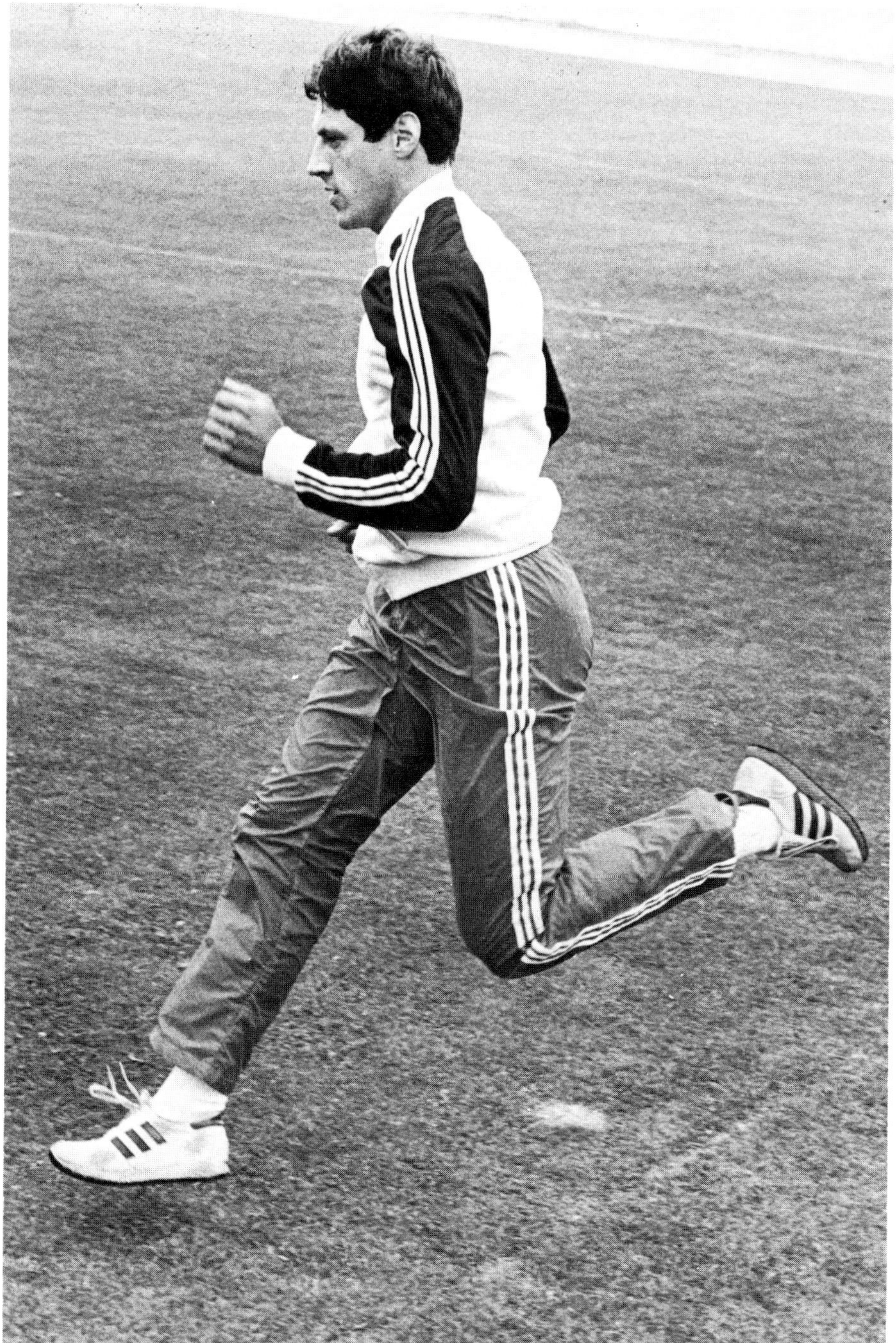

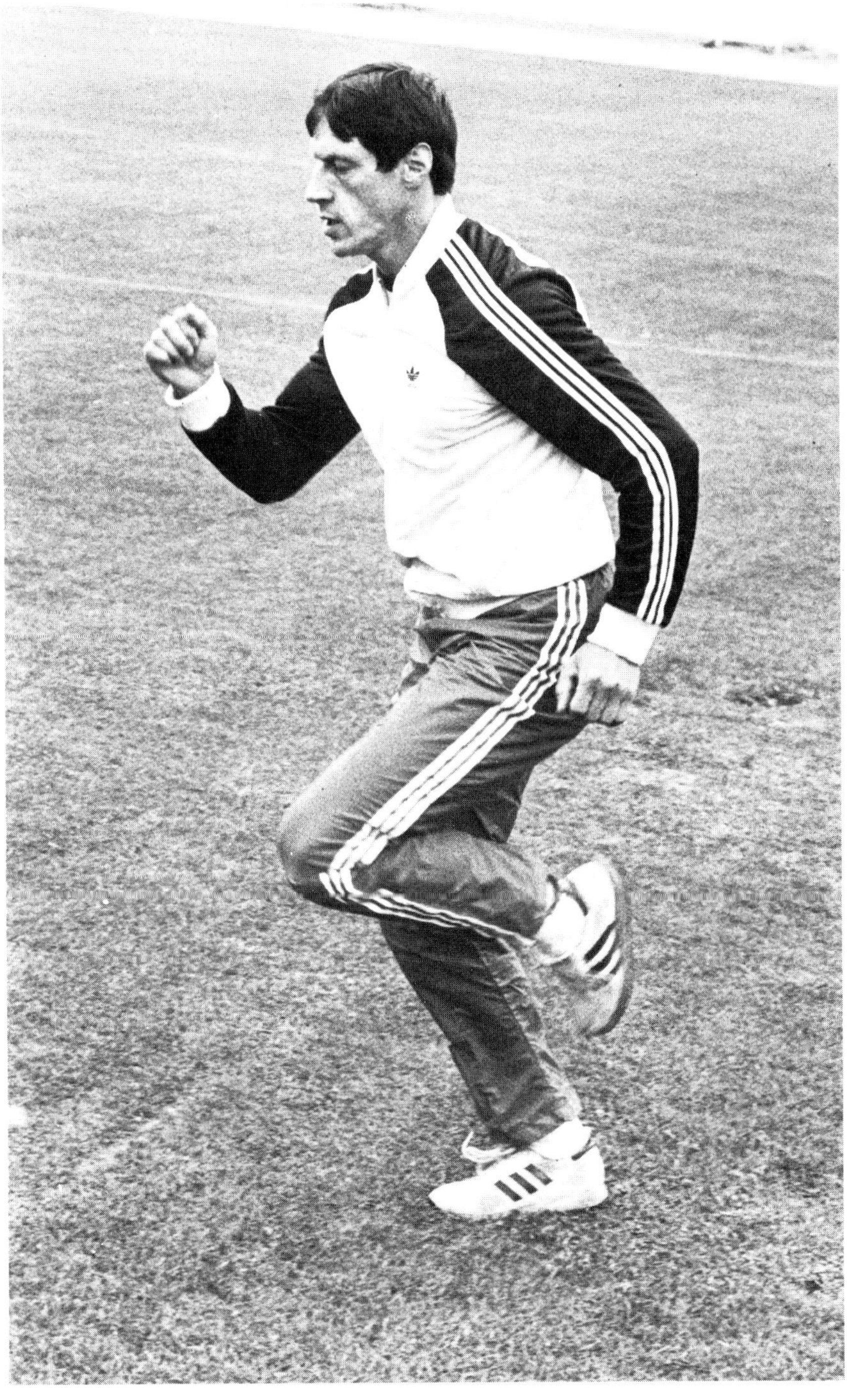

PREPARATION AND WARM-UP

Above and opposite: *In this exercise the head and neck pass through the full range of movement*

PREPARATION AND WARM-UP

*The arm and shoulder are lifted and stretched
without twisting the body*

Above and following page:
Push the hips forward, and then back, as far as possible

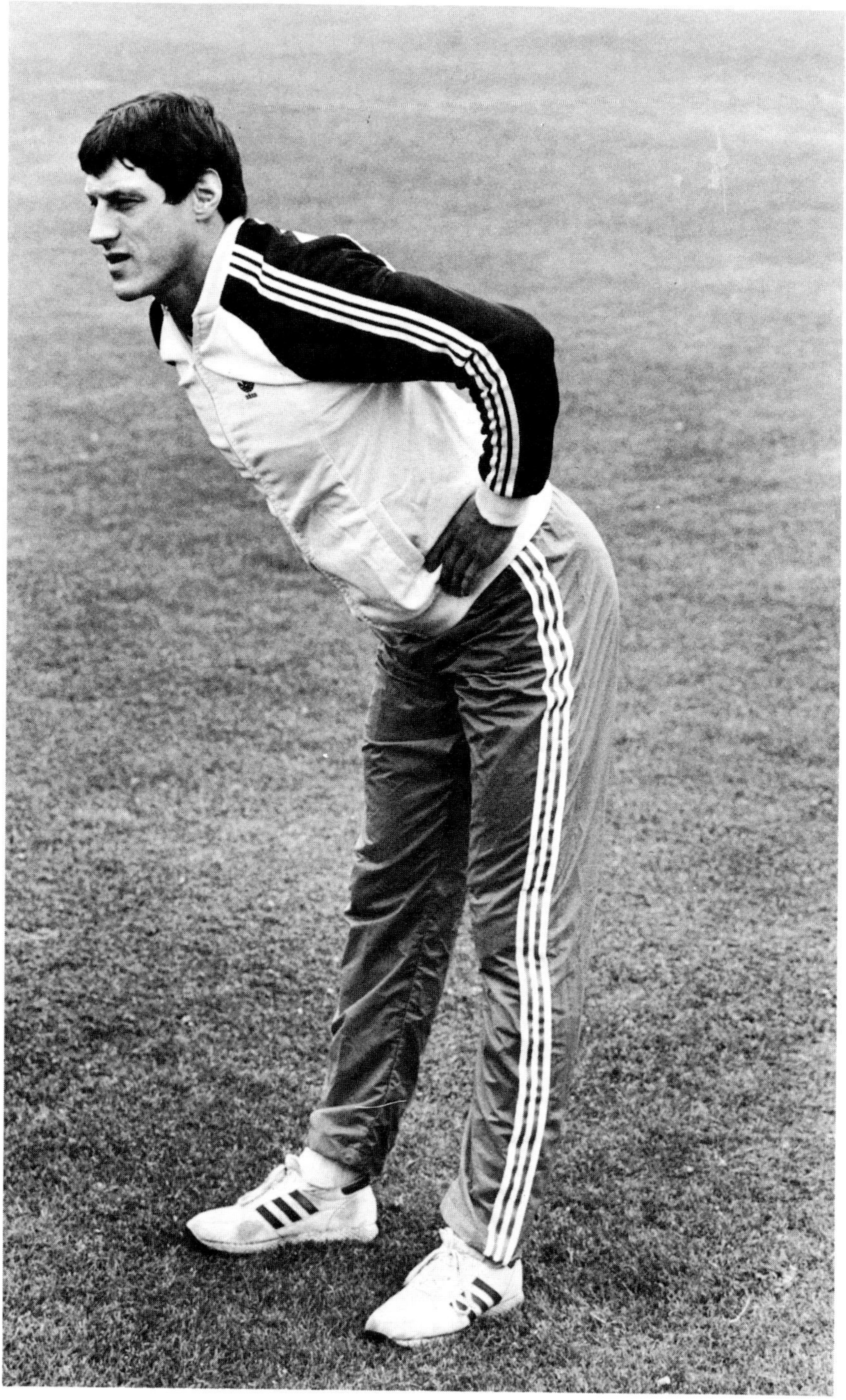

Above and following page: *Side bends: note the position of the shoulders; the torso must not bend forward*

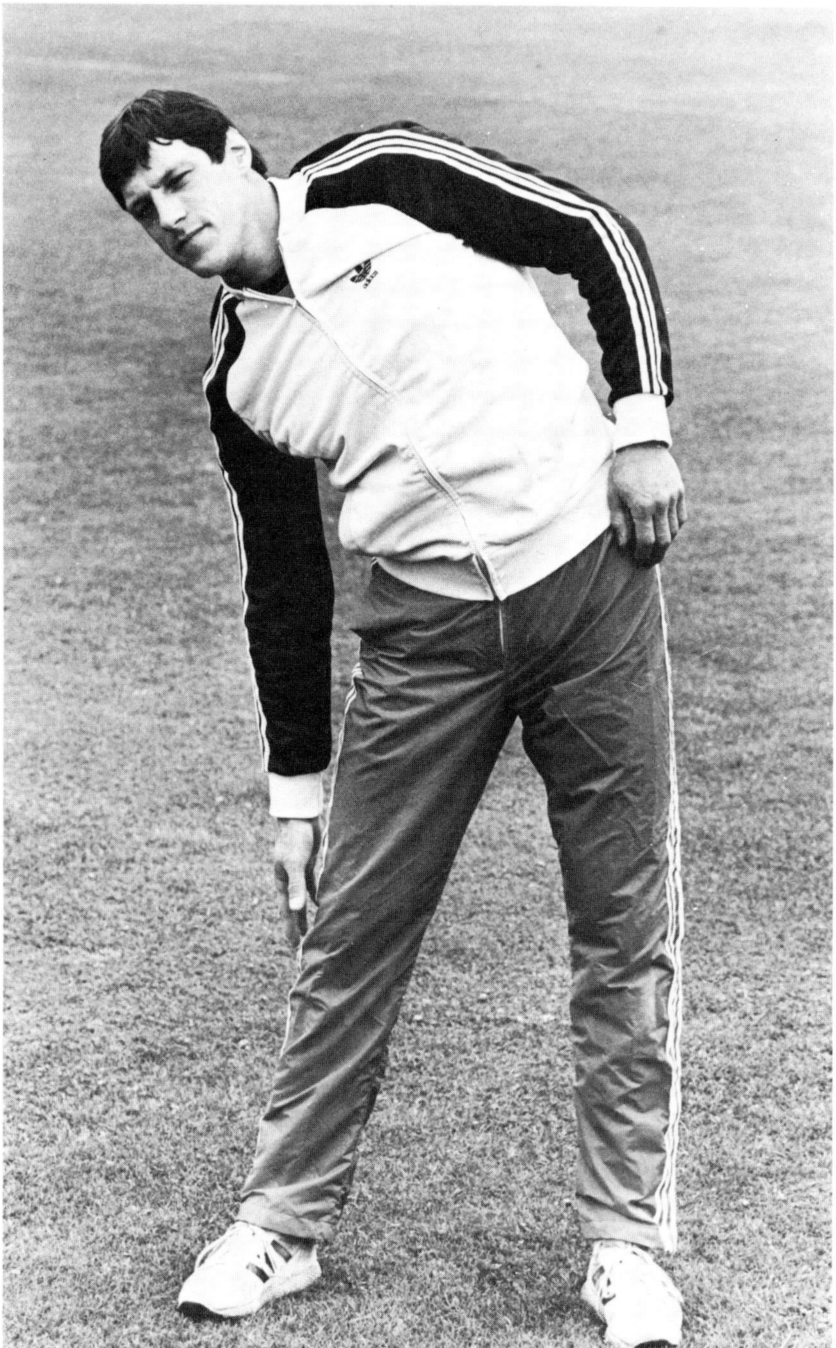

PREPARATION AND WARM-UP

A good straight calf stretch

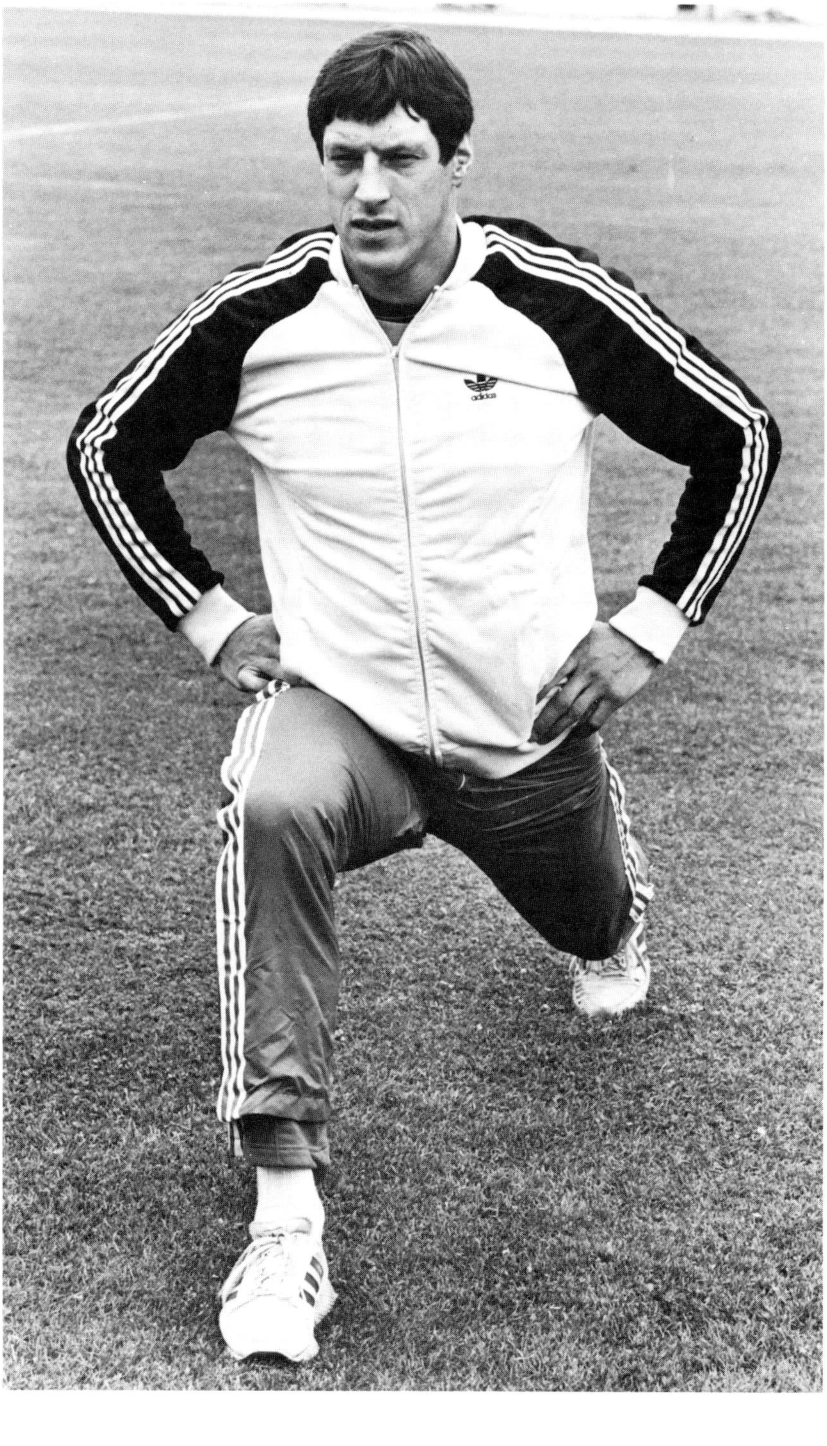

PREPARATION AND WARM-UP

Opposite and above:
Lunge exercise: note the position of the feet and the upright stance

PREPARATION AND WARM-UP

Above and opposite:
Lunge exercise with the rear foot on its side

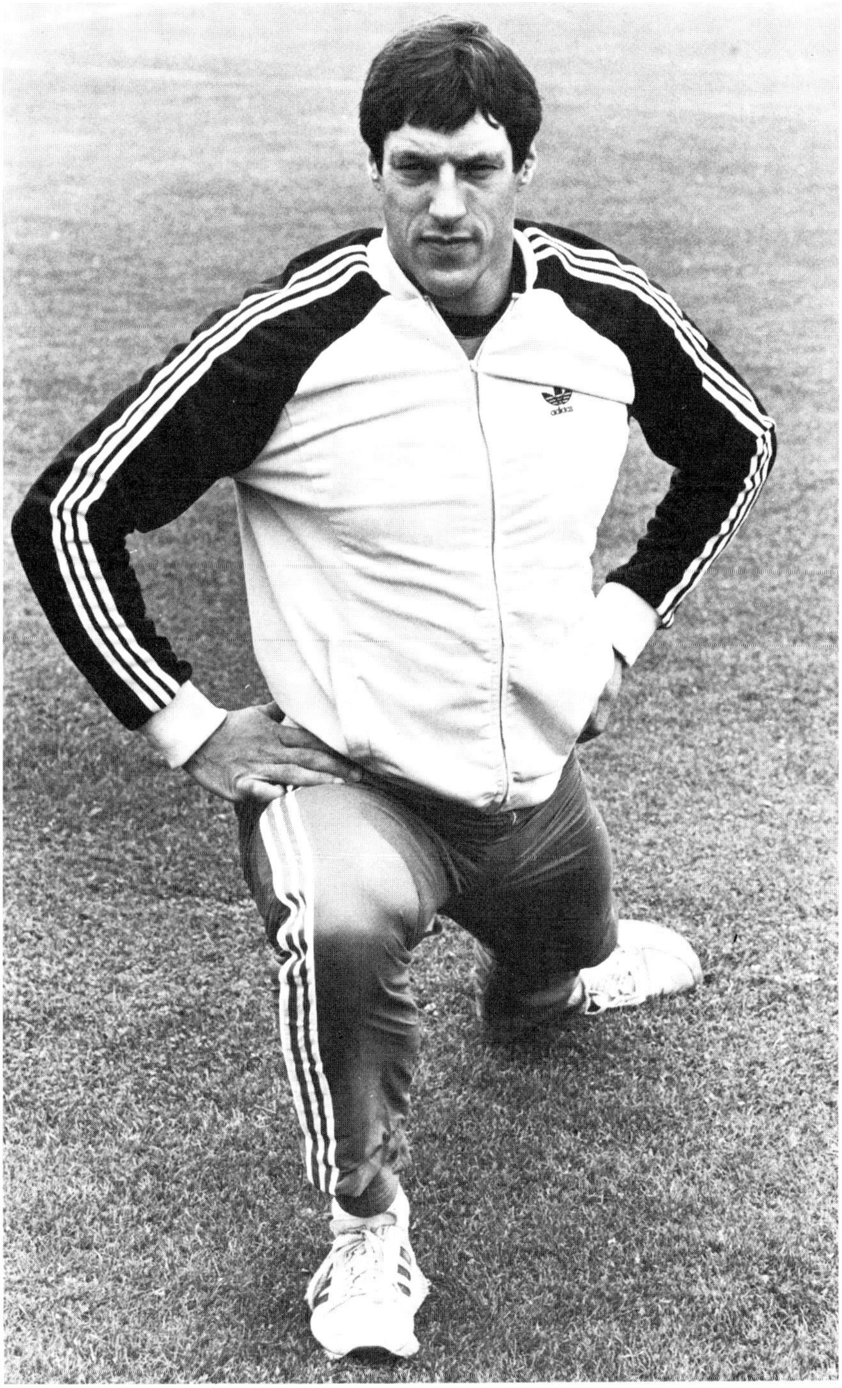

PREPARATION AND WARM-UP

An excellent stretch in which the muscle is not put under pressure

PREPARATION AND WARM-UP

*To achieve the maximum stretch, this position
of the foot is essential*

A good open position showing good mobility

CHAPTER FOUR

Technique

To describe sprinting as a technical event may come as a surprise to some people; but, as in other events, there are some fundamental similarities and a lot of personal differences. If we compare Allan's technique of sprinting with Don Quarrie's, we find that the leg action (i.e. the knee lift and extension) is similar, but the arm action is different and, therefore, the overall picture is totally different. One must also take into account the athlete's own strengths and weaknesses, as well as build, height, etc. All these factors affect the end product and determine the way a sprinter runs. If we look at Allan's physical attributes, we find he has a powerful physique and a lot of elastic strength, gained from his long-jumping days; he therefore runs in a sort of bounding fashion, using the track to power his way along it.

Arm and leg action

It is said that the arms control the legs. You will find that if you run with your arms swinging slowly by your side you move with a long slow stride, but if your arms have a short fast action then you will have a short fast stride. The ideal is somewhere in between. The arms should be held in a relaxed state with the shoulders down; at no time during the race should the shoulders be lifted as this creates tension in the upper body and neck and causes the athlete to slow down and tire at the end of a race. The hands must be in a relaxed, closed fist with the thumb on top (to prevent the arms going too far back) and with the elbow bent at a loose 90° angle. The arms should work straight backwards and forwards in a piston-like action with the emphasis on the backward and not the forward action. However, it will be noticed

page 44
pages 46, 47
48

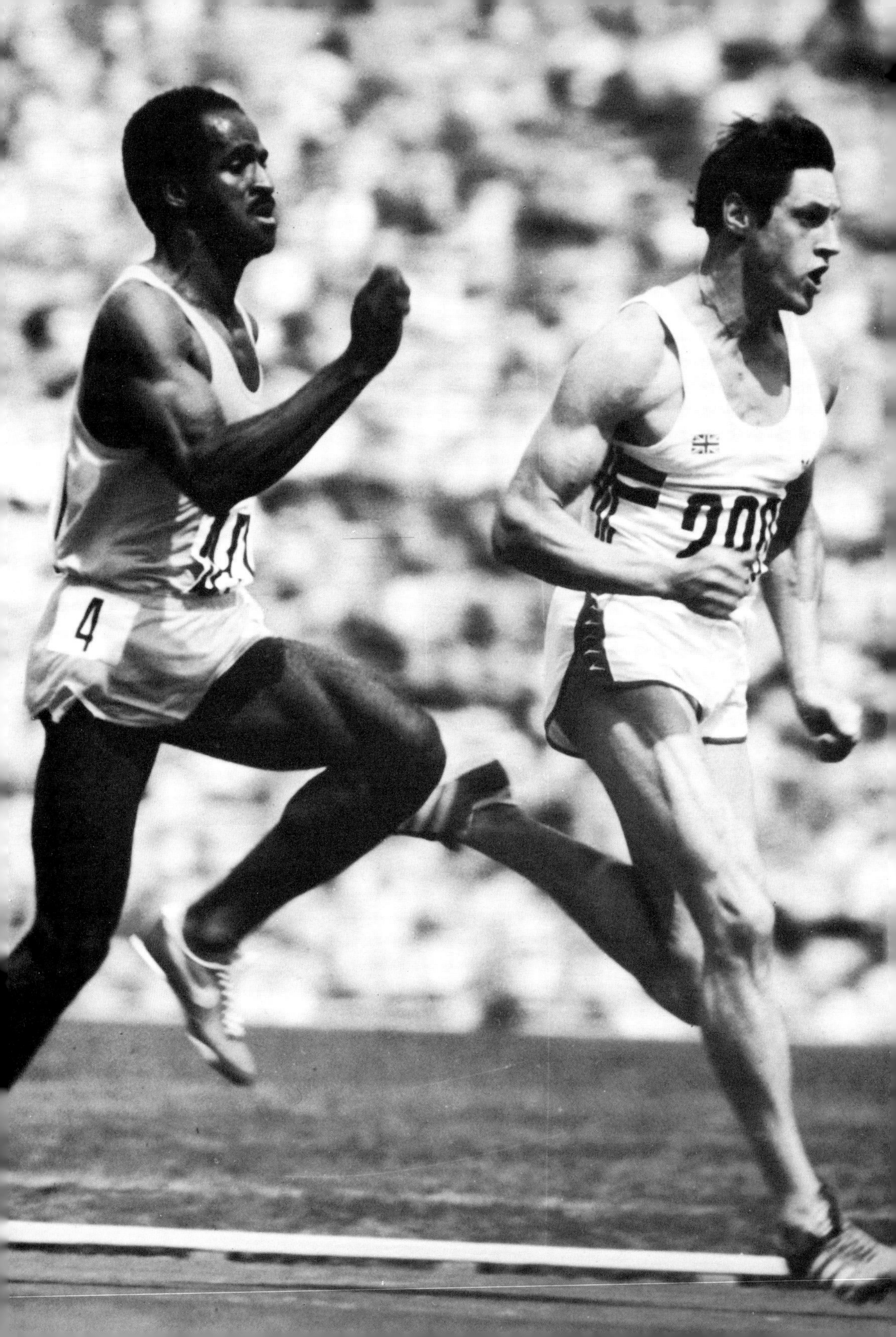
4

if one looks at Don Quarrie that he has a very high forward action which enables him to have a high knee lift; there are two completely different schools of thought, yet both actions produce world-class performances.

The legs have to concentrate on two things: (a) rapidity of movement and (b) length of stride. This tends to categorise sprinters into either cadence sprinters — i.e. runners who sprint by taking short, very fast strides — or power sprinters, who move their legs slightly slower but take long raking strides. Athletes in the first category include Houstan McTear, Pietro Mennea, Stanley Floyd and Mel Lattany. The power sprinters include Allan Wells, Valeri Borzov, Haseley Crawford, Frank Emmelmann and Eugen Ray. The sprinter has to work on both areas but will be predominantly inclined to one or the other. You should work hard at either (a) keeping the rate of stride steady and increasing the length or (b) keeping the length of stride steady and increasing the rate.

The leg should have a high knee action and, while maintaining this, should reach out and pull back at the ground in a type of paw-like movement. This must feel natural and must still resemble running. Too often, runners try to copy other people's technique when, in reality, it would not suit their type of body frame or natural style of running.

pages 49, 50 51, 52

The body lean should be produced by the pull back of the arms, but should not be exaggerated by going either too far back or too far forward. If the body lean is too far forward it will affect the legs by not allowing the knees to come up, producing the effect of running underneath oneself. If the lean is too far back then the right amount of backward drive cannot be achieved. It is therefore best to seek a happy medium.

Don Quarrie's high arm action contrasts with Allan's low relaxed carriage of the arms

TECHNIQUE

Above and following two pages:
Allan's relaxed but powerful use of his arms

TECHNIQUE

TECHNIQUE

TECHNIQUE

A good high knee lift is indispensible for successful sprinting

TECHNIQUE

Allan maintains knee lift while showing good extension

The relaxed recovery leg phase

The knee comes through high to begin another stride

TECHNIQUE

*After Allan's 200-metres victory
in Turin, 1979, he is pictured here with Pietro Mannea*

The correct body lean into the bend

TECHNIQUE

Bend running

Running on the turn can be one of the most pleasant experiences if done properly. The 200-metre is a sprint, and that means the athlete must learn to run flat out round the curve. In order to do this one must adapt the technique slightly by driving the right arm across the body to enable one to lean into the curve. Another important factor is to run as close to the line as possible, thus running the shortest distance; but possibly most important of all is the conservation of energy. Running the curve should be smooth, without spurts and cruises, as this only saps the energy and leaves the athlete too drained to run the straight without tiring badly. It has been said that it was impossible to run the bend as fast as Allan did and maintain that speed to the end. He proved it *was* possible in the 1981 200-metres in Berlin. Allan blasted his usual bend and kept going, pulling away from Lattany and Phillips of the U.S.A., to run 20.15 s on a very cold, wet evening at 11.00 p.m. Not ideal conditions, as you would surely agree!

The start and the finish

Once the body 'knows' how to sprint, and this technique has been adapted to the personal qualities of the athlete, two other important factors which affect a race have to be considered, that is the start and the finish. One is probably as important as the other in that races can be won or lost at either.

The start

Let us look first of all at the start. A pupil at school once asked me what was the point of getting down when all you had to do was get up again! Good point. Another good point is that if you cannot do a sprint start properly then you are as well standing up. The start is probably the most practised part of a sprinter's training. It begins when you are told to take off your tracksuit, because from that moment on you are under the starter's commands. After removing all outer garments, which should be left on until the direction is given, you will be called to stand 3 metres behind the line. This is the time to adjust shorts, socks, hair etc., not when the command 'on your marks'

'On your marks' — *note the straight arms and balanced position of the body with the weight forward on the fingers*

'Go' — *the back leg is straight, after driving away from the blocks; the body is at the correct angle*

TECHNIQUE

is given. When the starter says 'on your marks' all athletes must walk forward and go down together. This is often where gamesmanship will occur with one athlete standing up or moving around a bit while the others go down. Do not let this upset you, because if others are thinking of delaying tactics, their minds are not 100 per cent on the race, and the only person they are putting off is themselves.

Technical points

page 56

'On your marks'
1. Fingers bridged and behind the line, not touching
2. Arms straight
3. Shoulders over the hands
4. Head in natural alignment
5. Feet comfortable
6. One knee approximately opposite the instep of the other foot
7. Whole position should feel comfortable
8. When ready — remain motionless

'Set'
1. Hips are raised
2. Back leg should be bent
3. Weight pushed forward over hands, with shoulders in front of hands
4. Head still in alignment
5. This position, while steady, should not be able to be held for too long before causing too much pressure on the fingers

page 57

'Go'
1. The arm drives backwards
2. Head remains steady
3. The leg drives, and the first stride should come through low and fast. The action should resemble an aeroplane taking off

There are various thoughts on the stride pattern at the start. Some people believe in many short strides while others believe in fewer and longer strides. The aim at the start of the race is to start as fast as you can with as little energy expenditure as possible. This tends to support

*This award-winning photograph conveys the athletes'
power and determination as they drive away from the start in Moscow*

TECHNIQUE

the belief in longer and fewer strides. But the main aim, no matter how it is accomplished, is to start well and make the rest of the field chase you.

Blocks

At one time the question everyone was asking was whether or not to use blocks. That problem was solved by the I.A.A.F. ruling that starting blocks had to be used in competition, and I think that Allan Wells might have been the subject under discussion when this ruling was agreed. So how did the decision not to use blocks come about?

Note the angle of the block to the line

TECHNIQUE

Starting blocks were originally used on cinder and grass tracks and their purpose was to prevent the athletes slipping; with the new all-weather surfaces blocks were no longer necessary. Because of our track training methods, in which we have long rests between runs, we had constantly to keep picking up the blocks and resetting them before each run, as other people wanted to use the same lane. This became a rather tedious exercise, so, primarily out of a reluctance to keep re-measuring the mark for the blocks, we began to start without them and found that we got just as good a start. As we were no longer using them in training it was pointless using them for competition. The start without blocks was discovered, therefore, not through the wonders of science but through sheer laziness!

The only drawback we found was that there was no support behind to prevent the heel dropping, and no matter how strong the athlete, the heel will drop a fraction, thus losing valuable hundredths of a second.

On the introduction of the new law (which came as no surprise) we did not technically alter the start at all; we just had to make a slight adjustment in the distance of the front foot from the starting line. Later on we tried one block and found this was ideal for Allan, as it prevented his heel from dropping and ensured a secure position whilst still allowing him to get closer to the starting line. This method was also vetoed by the I.A.A.F., and he now has to use both blocks as laid down by the new rules.

Starting on the bend

The technique of the start is the same as for running on the straight but the difference lies in the positioning of the blocks. In order to run the bend in a straight line and in an economical fashion, the blocks are set at an angle. If this were not done the athlete would have to run straight and then cut into the curve, causing him to use up a lot of energy and break up his stride pattern.

The finish

The dip is a controversial area and it is debatable whether it is an advantage to hold form and run through, or whether to dip for the line, thus losing form but at the same time perhaps gaining valuable

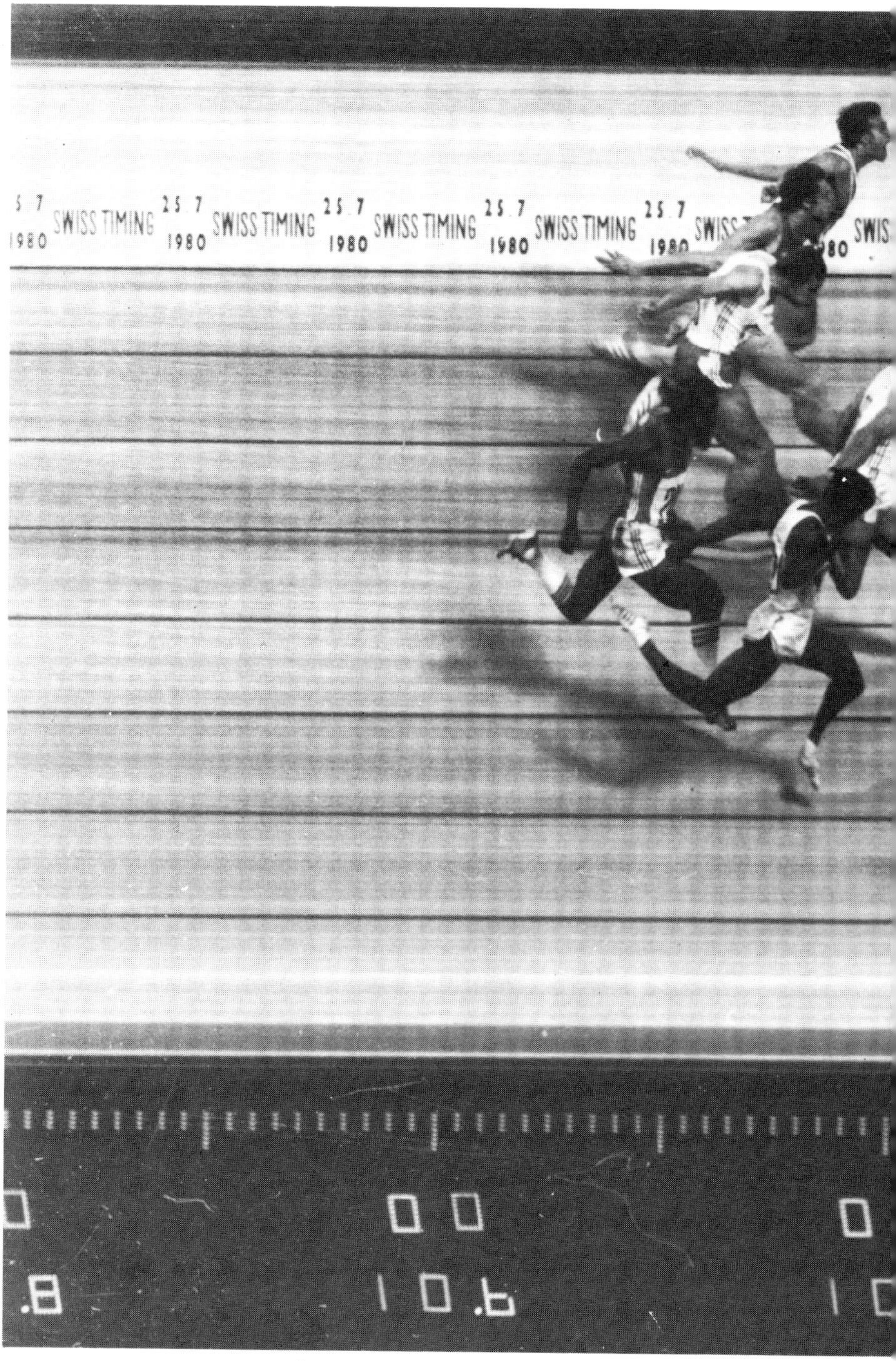
SWISS TIMING
25.7
1980

*This photo-finish of the Olympic 100-metres in Moscow
shows Allan timing the dip to perfection*

TECHNIQUE

inches. The important factor regarding the dip is its timing. If you dip too soon then, by losing form and leaning forward, you will slow down and lose the advantage you should have gained. As it is the torso that counts as you cross the line, it is important not to stick your head out, as this has the effect of pushing the chest backwards. The technique must be right. It is impossible to practise the dip except under race conditions, so you may lose a couple of races until you learn when is the right time to dip and how best to do it. The important thing is to learn from each race and to understand what is the right thing for *you* to do, rather than to copy other people.

CHAPTER FIVE

Training

As I said in an earlier chapter, each person trains differently as each person is built differently, has different facilities and different thoughts on the subject. I propose, therefore, to discuss some of the methods we use to train and some we do not.

General training methods

Our training year is split into four sections — two gym sessions and two track sessions. The only difference between the first and second gym and track sessions is their length. The first gym sessions last approximately six weeks and track sessions approximately twelve weeks, while the second sessions in the lead-up to the summer last eight and twenty-four weeks respectively. The gym sessions take the form of a type of circuit training.

Circuit training is normally seen as part of a winter training schedule and usually consists of a series of exercises done on a rotation basis. Our circuit consists of only four exercises. Why the difference? We feel that in doing our four exercises we can cover all the muscle groups necessary for sprinting and, therefore, there is no need to do any more.

The basic principle behind the training is overload at speed. In other words we ask the body to go through a greater range and endurance level than it ever has to during a race. In this way we build up a very high level of general sprinting fitness.

The exercises we use in our circuit are as follows:
(a) Speedball (which I will discuss in detail later on) *page 68*
(b) Chinnies — A form of sit-up. The body jack-knifes in the middle *pages 69, 70*

TRAINING

page 71

pages 72, 73

        with one knee crossing to the opposite shoulder. The hands are locked behind the head.

(c) Press-ups — The body should be in a straight line with the shoulders over the hands.

(d) Squats — Feet should be about 450 mm (18 in) apart facing straight forward. The knees bend over the feet while the back is kept as straight as possible.

These exercises are done on a rotation system and, depending on the length of time in the gym, are performed from two to six times. For example:

Week 2
Speedball   6 × 40 chinnies 6 × 20 press-ups 6 × 30 squats
Week 6
Speedball   3 × 100 chinnies 3 × 50 press-ups 3 × 50 squats

By the end of the gym session the body is extremely fit and one is ready to move on to the track for a completely different type of work. This type of training is very hard, both physically and mentally, as every night the body is pushed to the limit and the mind has counted and re-counted numerous exercises. Training is also hard mentally in that one knows it is going to hurt before one starts, which does not help.

    Our work on the track differs from most, in that once the preliminary build-up sessions, lasting five weeks, are over, we never run over distance, and the majority of our work is done from the blocks. In this way we are setting up a race situation time and time again, thus recreating the same physical demands as in a race. Obviously to recreate the mental and nervous state would be wrong as the athlete would very quickly be exhausted, and the actual race would be nothing new. The five-week build-up consists of running over varying distances, gradually building up in speed. The same session is done for a whole week. For example:

Week 1
2 × (6 × 100 metres) at 65 per cent effort
with walk back recovery between runs and fifteen minutes between sets.
Week 2
2 × (6 × 60 metres) at 75 per cent effort

TRAINING

and so on, gradually getting faster until we eventually run flat out and graduate from a standing start to starting blocks.

Many sprinters leave most of their sprinting behind them on the training track, and, consequently, when they come to race their legs are heavy and performances are below par. Therefore a sprinter's training should consist of short, very fast, runs, with a long recovery between each run. In this way each run is of the highest quality and although there will be a small fall-off in times, this should not be any more than a few hundredths of a second. For example, 3×60 metres with five minutes recovery or $2 \times (4 \times 30$ metres) with walk back recovery and ten minutes between sets.

If, on reading this, you are asking yourself when do we do repetition 150 metres or 300 metres, then the answer is, we don't! Fitness to run comes from the gym phase and therefore we only use the track to get 'track-fit'. On completion of the 'track-fitness' we then get 'race-fit'. This is done by running trials over 100 metres and 200 metres and, in this way, we get ready to race.

At world-class level an athlete needs to train twice a day and, therefore, the session in the morning has to be a different type of work-out. In the gym phase the training day is split thus:

	a.m.	p.m.
Gym fitness	power work	circuit training
	bounding, hopping etc.	speedball gym work
Track fitness	a.m.	p.m.
	power work	track work
	bounding	60s, 30s etc.

As I have already explained the evening sessions, let us turn to the morning sessions — power work. This is a totally different type of training which is incorporated into most athletes' training programmes. The type of power essential to sprinters is elastic strength, as opposed to the brute strength of a shot putter. While making the body stronger, one must at the same time introduce the recoil factor into the muscle.

Various exercises in this field follow.

The speedball: exercise no. 1 in the circuit

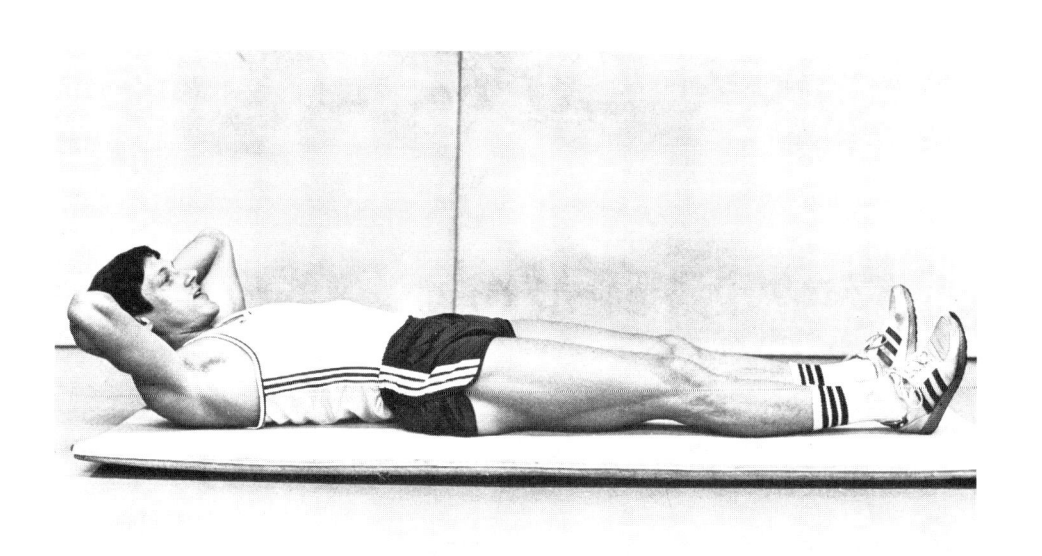

The starting position for chinnies

Above and following page: *Side and front views of the body jack-knifing, as the knee crosses the chest*

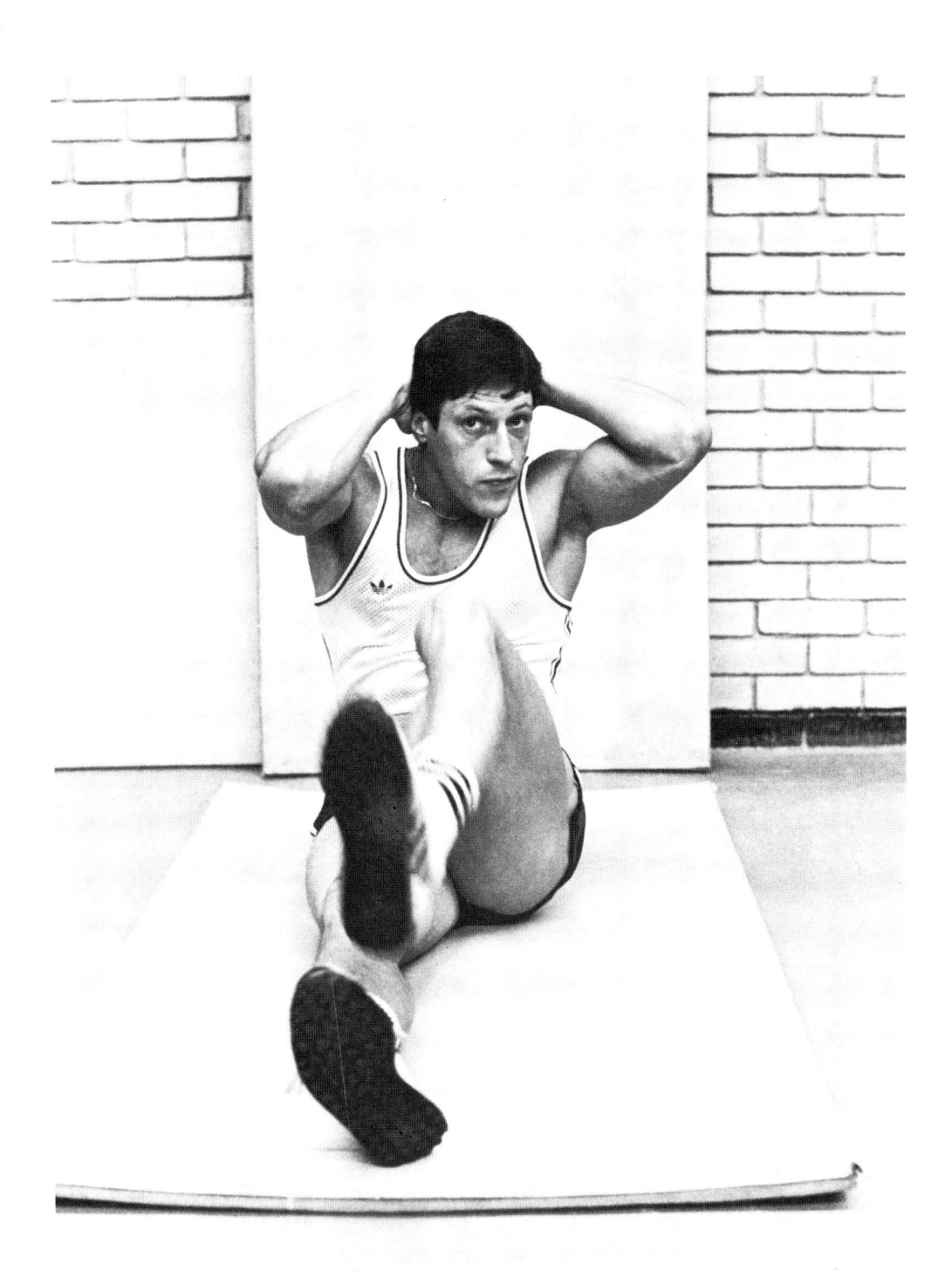

The body must remain absolutely straight throughout the press-up

The starting and finishing position of the squat — the feet apart and facing forward

A good squatting position: note the straight back

TRAINING

Bounding

pages 76, 77 Bounding, the best-known of these exercises, is a form of elongated running steps with the aim of covering as much distance as possible. This is done by leaving the driving leg behind the body as long as possible, while holding the knee up in the air. Bounding should be done over a variety of distances and at varying speeds. It is often done also on varying gradients, but should always be done on grass as the ankles and knees take a lot of pounding. Bounding on hard surfaces could lead to injuries.

Hopping

Hopping is done over short distances and for speed. Although one should try to cover as much distance as possible this should not reduce the speed of the hops. A good exercise is to count the number of hops taken over a certain distance and try to reduce this number as you progress. The hopping surface should be flat and grassy, again to prevent injuries.

High knee stepping

pages 78, 79 This is used to try to prevent the high knee lift from dropping at the end of a race. It is a form of running produced by taking very short steps while bringing the knees up as high as possible on each step.

Deep-knee jumping

Otherwise known as 'bunny-jumps'. This involves jumping from two feet in a crouch position and landing in the same position.

Another form of this is 'depth-jumping' where the athlete jumps from a height on one box and rebounds to land on top of another box at a different height.

Hill running

page 80 If possible this session should be done on grass. A golf course is ideal if you can get permission to use it; dodging the balls may improve your

TRAINING

speed! The length of the run should vary depending on the incline of the hill. In other words, if the incline is extremely steep then the distance should be short and if the incline is slight then you should run over a greater distance. Technique should never be neglected while running up hills, and the runs, especially over a short distance, should be as fast as possible. Running on hills is a good way of strengthening the drive of the arms and improving knee lift and drive in the legs.

Weight training

The most common strength work-out is weight training. Although Allan used this type of training when he was long-jumping, he has never used weights since changing his event to sprinting. The main reason was that he found a more than adequate substitute in the speedball. However, 90 per cent of all athletes use weights, so they must have a purpose. If we were to use weights for sprinting then we would use light weights doing fast repetitions. This is all I am going to say on this subject as I do not feel qualified to expand on weight training when weights are not used as part of our programme and when there are so many experts in this field.

TRAINING

Allan demonstrates his past long-jump training

TRAINING

Power work during a morning work-out

Above and opposite: *High knee stepping: note the straight back; how, too, the arms help the knee lift by pumping high into the air*

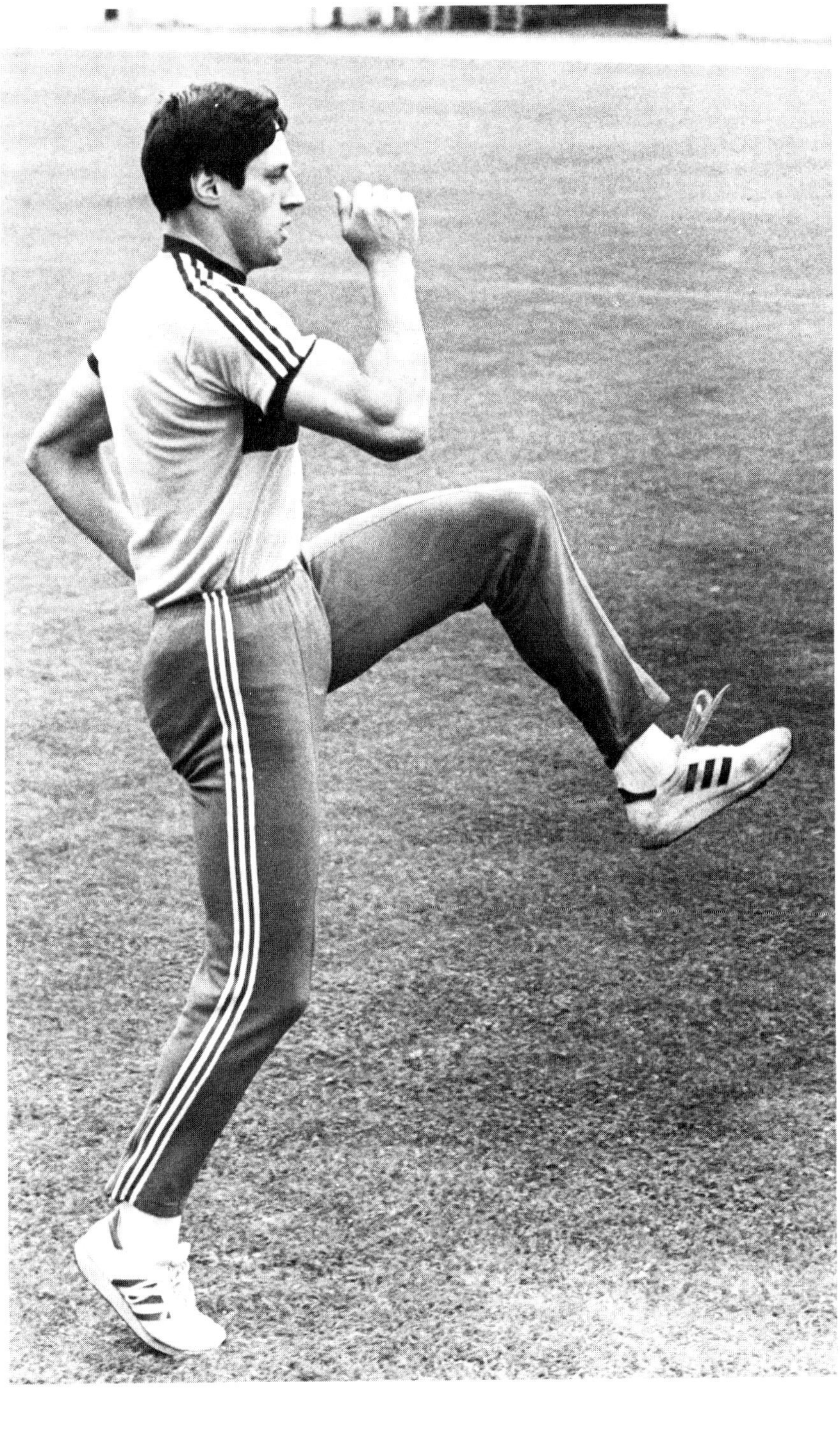

TRAINING

Hill-running — a variation in power work

The speedball

I have mentioned the speedball on numerous occasions throughout this book without really explaining what it is or its purpose in a sprinter's programme. First of all it is not a magic wand and secondly it is not an arm exercise! The speedball is a refined version of a boxer's punchball. It is suspended from a solid board on a swivel joint and can move backwards and forwards and from side to side. The hands must be protected by leather padded mitts, otherwise the hands and knuckles become cut, making them too sore to hit the ball.

pages 82, 83 84

The purpose of hitting the ball is to gain upper body strength and at the same time to improve concentration, cross-body co-ordination, reflexes and maximum relaxation while working flat out. The swinging ball is hit alternately with either hand with a form of punching action, and although the ball is hit with the hands, the movement starts in the feet and works its way up the body, finishing by hitting the ball. If at any time you tense up then you will miss the ball and, in this way, the athlete can practise working as fast as possible without tensing the shoulders and arms. As the ball moves extremely fast, the brain has to send messages to the muscles much faster than it would have to during a race and so when the athlete comes to race, the body has already been conditioned to move at speed. Not only does this help in the preparation for running fast but it also helps to cut out the injury risk. The major drawback when hitting the speedball is the noise it makes, although this also has its benefits. As the ball is moving at great speed, it becomes impossible to sight the ball and one must concentrate on its sound. As you can imagine, this becomes extremely difficult when more than one person is hitting the ball at one time. Concentration must be one hundred per cent in order to keep the ball going.

Sessions done on the ball vary in time and number, but the athlete must try to hit the ball faster each time.

TRAINING

Above, opposite and following page:
The speedball: the technique of hitting the ball

TRAINING

TRAINING

TRAINING

Sprint training for women

The principles behind sprint training for women are basically the same as for men. Although women have a different shape, physique and power/weight ratio this only means that they should limit the total number of repetitions of an exercise or the total number of jumps or bounds done in a session. A world-class woman sprinter has to be as good as an average male sprinter and, for this reason, I believe that a woman should run and train like a man. Billie-Jean King once said that the reason she was so successful was that she played a man's game of tennis, so I tried to run the same way as Allan and did exactly the same training, although with fewer reps and less distance on the power work.

In the gym phase of our training I never asked for, and was never given, any special consideration because I was a woman, even though I was the first woman to go right through this form of training. When I started I could only do two press-ups, but through the years I have managed to build up to a set of fifty, which would shame a lot of men. I achieved this simply by practice, every day and sometimes twice a day. The chinnies exercise I found to be no problem and managed to do a thousand, the same as, if not more than, some of the lads I trained with. The speedball was the one exercise in which I could not keep up with them, but even then my score was much higher than other well-established British male sprinters outside our own training group. I was not able to do as many bounds in the power sessions, but on the hill sessions I always did the same number of runs, albeit a little slower, but still at my maximum level.

On the track, because we used a handicap system, I inevitably found myself running as the hare, and when you have someone chasing you who sounds like a steam train, it can be a bit intimidating. My main problem was that, for most of the time, I trained with men and, therefore, I tried harder to stay in front; when I came up against women, I did not always try as hard.

It is unfair to compare my performances with the training, as I gradually became more involved with Allan's training and so my performance tailed off slightly. But from being a 12.1 s 100-metre sprinter I improved to 11.4 and was a Commonwealth Games semi-finalist in the 100-metre and 200-metre. As the form of training

TRAINING

described here has worked for Allan, so has it worked for me, and would work for any other woman. The thing one has to remember is that each individual's make-up is different: no form of training can alter that. If you do not have all the mental and physical qualities that go into making a world-class sprinter then although training will go a long way towards compensating for this lack, it cannot do everything.

On the technical side of sprinting I was always given the same advice as Allan, but there are several schools of thought on the subject. Lots of women run with a very fast cadence rate and a very low arm action, with the arm moving across the body rather than backwards and forwards. Marlies Gohr is a good example of this. Her coach also trained Renate Stecher who had a very powerful action. One must conclude that the running action of a woman, as in a man, is decided by the attributes of the runner; perhaps this is where I was given the wrong advice.

Women are now doing sub-11 second performances quite regularly and therefore their training schedules are very similar to those of some men. In fact, one East German coach said that the women in his squad could cope with long reps much better than the men, and all the squad were international athletes. Gone are the days when women just ran for fun and went to training either to eye up the local talent or to see their friends! Women must now train and race as hard as their male counterparts, and there is nothing in this book that women could not cope with, as I have tried and tested it all for them.

Renate Stecher exemplifies the difference in build and power

Marlies Gohr: a sprinter with a fairly light build but extremely fast leg action

The coach's relationship with the athlete does not always have to be this close!

CHAPTER SIX

The mental approach

At world-class level it is probably the athlete with the best mental approach on the day who will win the race. At this level successful sprinting is probably ninety per cent mental attitude and ten per cent physical fitness. For this reason a sprinter can become extremely tired at the end of a season, not because he has physically exhausted himself but because the mental preparation has left him drained. In the early stages of an athlete's career ambition is often the motivating factor; the stimulus is the desire to run for your country. On achieving this vest, one then aims to run for Great Britain, in the Commonwealth Games, European Games and Olympic Games. So as the athlete improves he is continually setting his sights higher.

Most athletes consider it an achievement just to run in the Olympic Games, but when there is a chance of winning, one's mental attitude is completely different. The athlete who sets out to *get* to the Games is relaxed, knowing he has achieved his aim, and although he will attempt to do his best, he knows that he is just trying to get through as many rounds as possible. What of the pressures on the athlete who is expected to win a medal? This breed of sprinter has to have the ability to remain calm and mentally to reduce the greatness of the occasion to an ordinary club meeting with a few hundred spectators. He must learn to use the occasion to his advantage while, at the same time, never underestimating the performance of his competitors.

Athletes often make the mistake of making claims about their performances before a race, and in this way put themselves under pressure to live up to these claims. It is far better to be cautious and surprise people, than to say you are going to win and be wrong. Winning a race, especially in sprints, is rarely a foregone conclusion, as sometimes only a metre can separate first from last. For this reason the athlete is under greater mental pressure than in any other event.

THE MENTAL APPROACH

The sprinter must be ready to react whenever the starter calls him to his marks; he has no time to build up alertness during a race. In order to be ready, his concentration before the race must be of the highest quality. Other athletes may try to put him off by talking or shaking hands but, while remaining polite, he should not enter into long conversations as this will only distract him from the job ahead. The psychology of the sprint often leads to athletes saying things or shouting comments; they are really trying to scare opponents into running badly. If the sprinter gets worked up and angry then his adrenalin will get going too early, which will result in loss of energy. If other athletes want to say things about you, let them; it is a compliment in a way as it shows they are worried about you!

Other pressures come from the media and the public, in that a lot of people think that all one has to do to win is appear on the track. Nothing is further from the truth. A sprint race is never a foregone conclusion and never will be, by the nature of the event. A split-second loss of concentration in the middle of a race could cost a metre. Sprinting demands total concentration and tunnel vision from start to finish, and this approach must be developed in training. The athlete who looks for the opposition will soon find it, passing him! Total concentration is difficult to achieve unless it is practised in training as well as in competition. Training should be disciplined and well-drilled. One does not go to training to have a good time and a laugh; training must be an enjoyable experience, but it is a physical enjoyment as opposed to an emotional one like watching a good film. The athlete must perfect the art of excluding all noise and distractions, and learn to build himself up into a state of readiness for the task ahead.

The main aim is to give the best performance possible; and if, at the end of the day, you achieve this and someone beats you, then it is hard lines and you will just have to train a bit harder the next time. Your total concern during a race should be for yourself; it does not matter who else is in the race or what times have been done before, it is what is done on that day which is all-important. Never try to beat a particular person in the race; you must consider *everyone* as a threat and run the race to the best of your ability.

The coach should play an important role in the psychological aspect of an athlete's training. It is up to him to ensure that the training

THE MENTAL APPROACH

facilities are the best possible, that all equipment needed is provided, that other athletes are there to train with and that there is a good competitive spirit within the squad. It is also important that he should get to know the athlete and be interested not only in his performance but also in the person himself. He must understand what makes him tick and what motivates him. The coach must not take too much responsibility away from the athlete, because at the end of the day he is on his own during a race, the coach is not always present to advise him and tell him what to do. Therefore, part of the coach's job should be to help the athlete to develop into a thinking person with his own views on training and racing. Throughout an athlete's career, as he improves, he will learn a lot about himself and a lot from other athletes; it is the job of the coach to listen and to develop the training and the coach/athlete relationship accordingly. His role should combine that of coach and advisor, but above all he should be a friend and companion.

When all is said and done, whether you make it to the top, stop in the middle, or never leave the bottom, if when you look back on your career you can say that you tried your best, enjoyed yourself and reached the limit of your potential, then you can retire satisfied and complete, not only as an athlete, but as a person.

I leave you with two main ideals, not only applicable to sprinting but to athletics in general:

1. Athletics is simple — do not try to make it complicated. The easier it is the better.
2. Enjoy yourself — time in athletics is short in terms of years of your life, and there are so many people who go around saying 'I could have been good if I had tried'. Do not become one of them. You have been given a talent, and it is your duty — and opportunity — to exploit that talent to the full.

Allan shows great concentration before a race

An interview with Allan Wells

Q. Do you still have an interest in long jumping as an event?
A. Only in that it holds a special place in my athletic career from an early age.

Q. Do you think you would ever return to long jumping?
A. I have always felt that since taking up sprinting I have not fulfilled my potential as a long jumper and, for this reason, I would like to return to this event some time in the future.

Q. Why do you think long jumping in this country has remained static since the days of Lynn Davies?
A. Long jumping is a specialised event; therefore it needs a person with a great deal of character and a lot of commitment. There have been jumpers with the same ability as Lynn but I feel they have lacked the commitment to take them to the top.

Q. Do you regret not having switched to sprinting earlier?
A. No, there is the thought that sprinters are relatively young when they reach their peak, but I would not change anything I have done over the past few years.

Q. Why do you think it took Great Britain 20 years to produce a world-class sprinter?
A. For many years Britain took it for granted that sprinters were American and Black. It also took a training method which was directly related to the event to bring out the best in the runners.

Q. What special qualities do you think a world-class sprinter needs to possess in order to cope with competing at a high level?
A. An individual needs commitment, motivation, tremendous fitness, confidence and the character to see through somewhat intimidating circumstances.

AN INTERVIEW WITH ALLAN WELLS

Q. Why do sprinters not hold a peak as long as middle- or long-distance runners?

A. Sprinting has a bigger element of nervous tension and is more physical and explosive than the other track events. Therefore, it is much harder to hold a mental and physical peak for a long time.

Q. It has been said that you have been the most consistent sprinter over the last four years. To what do you attribute your consistency?

A. Probably the way I train and also the way I build up to races — choosing the right races and peaking at the right time.

Q. Which performance do you regard as your best technically and which gave you the most pleasure?

A. There are so many runs that have been very good, but I would say that the 100-metres, second round in Moscow was the one which stood out above the rest. The most pleasurable run for me was undoubtedly the 100-metres final in Moscow.

Q. What would you consider was your greatest disappointment in athletics?

A. Probably the fact that I did not run to form in Prague.

Q. What is it about your event that the general public would find hard to understand?

A. Possibly the kind of concentrated commitment needed throughout the season, not only in competition but also in day-to-day training. Also the amount of nervous tension needed to gain maximum control and effort when starting from the blocks.

Q. Being Olympic champion brings with it enormous pressures from both the media and the public. Do you feel these are justified, and how do you cope with the burden?

A. As far as the media are concerned you grow into the pressured side of athletics as you improve, and you always have the option of speaking or not. Pressure is the sort of thing that goes hand in hand with success and therefore because I enjoy the success I put up with pressure.

Q. You are known as a big-time sprinter in that you always save your best performances for the big occasion. Is it because you enjoy the challenge, or do you have to limit your peak performances to so many per year?
A. It is a bit of both; mentally I build up over long periods for the big occasion, pacing myself up to a peak.

Q. A lot has been said about 'open' athletics. What are your views on the subject?
A. Open athletics is knocking on your doorstep. My only reservation is that I hope that it is properly controlled and brought about sensibly, in a way that will benefit both the mature athlete and the up-and-coming athlete of tomorrow.

Q. Finally, what advice would you give an up-and-coming sprinter?
A. It is difficult to give general advice, but I would say that you have to be single-minded, extremely fit and must always concentrate on your technique. It helps if you have a coach who understands the needs of the event as well as your individual needs, and who understands you and can motivate you as an athlete.

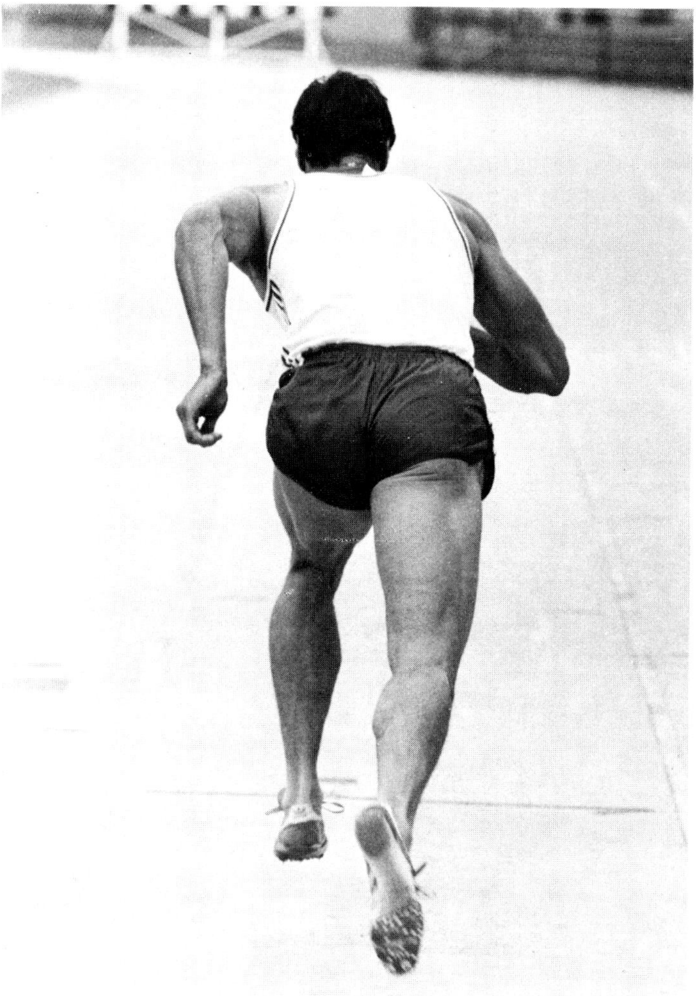